PRACTICAL

THOROUGH BASS,

or the

ART OF PLAYING FROM A FIGURED BASS

on the

Organ or Piano Forte,

BY

WM CROTCH, Mus. Doc.

Professor of Music in the University of Oxford,

and Principal of the Royal Academy of Music, London.

Pr 12 -

London

Published by CRAMER ADDISON & BEALE 201, Regent Street,
and 67, Conduit Street.

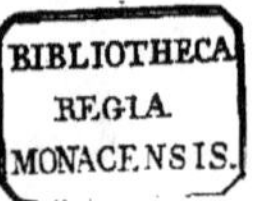
BIBLIOTHECA
REGIA
MONACENSIS.

CONTENTS.

INDEX TO THE EXAMPLES.

PRACTICAL THOROUGH BASS,

&c. &c.

Thorough Bass is the art of playing from figures, and was first regularly explained and arranged by Viadana early in the seventeenth century.

The present work is intended as a companion to the author's Elements of Composition, which include the whole theory of the subject.

He who understands harmony must understand thorough bass, though he may not be able to perform it; while the thorough bass player cannot even comprehend what he has to do without some knowledge of the rules of composition. A person may compose who cannot play at all. In this sense, thorough bass differs from composition. It is the habit of playing an extempore accompaniment to a given bass, or treble and bass, by the aid of figures; and this art therefore requires a command of the instrument, an eye capable of reading quickly, and a retentive memory. For the exercise and improvement of all these, a work, consisting of a concentration of the practical rules agreeing with the former theory, rejecting all that is foreign to this purpose, and containing a variety of practices and specimens, was required by the author's pupils, and others who approve of his method. With this sole view it is now produced, and not with the slightest intention of depreciating many excellent cotemporary works on the same subject.

The student having been taught his notes*, may first be required to play Example 1. He must then learn to reckon the semitones in any interval, thus from A to B are two semitones (or one tone); from B to C is one semitone, &c. And in the latter part of the same example, from F♭♭ to C♭♭ is seven semitones; from C♭♭ to G♭♭, seven semitones; and so of the rest—Ex. 1 and 2. In playing from a figured bass, the figures stand for treble notes, to be played with the right hand, and are to be always reckoned upwards from the bass note inclusive. Thus, if the bass note is A, the figure 2 stands for B, 3 for C, &c. as far as 9; no double figures, as 10, 11, 12, being in common use. If the base note is B, 2 represents C, 3 D, &c. &c. A 10th is written 3, as also a 17th; and thus 4 stands for 11 and 18, and 5 for 12 and 19, &c. &c.

A diatonic scale is a series of notes in alphabetical order, as the natural or white keys of the piano forte, or any scale which resembles them, viz. all such scales as are characterized by the flats and sharps placed at the beginning of the stave—Ex. 3. Diatonic intervals are such as can be performed on any diatonic scale, and are as follows:

				Naturals.
A	minor	2nd equal to	1 semitone.	Ex. 4, such as EF, or BC.
A	major	2nd ————	2 semitones.	5, ———— CD, DE, FG, GA, and AB
A	minor	3rd ————	3 semitones.	6, ———— AC, BD, DF, and EG.
A	major	3rd ————	4 semitones.	7, ———— CE, FA, and GB.
A	perfect	4th ————	5 semitones.	8, ———— CF, DG, EA, GC, AD, BE.
A superflous or extreme sharp		4th ————	6 semitones.	9, ———— FB.
An imperfect or extreme flat		5th ————	6 semitones.	10, ———— BF.
A	perfect	5th ————	7 semitones.	11, ———— CG, DA, EB, FC, GD, AE.
A	minor	6th ————	8 semitones.	12, ———— BG, AF, EC.
A	major	6th ————	9 semitones.	13, ———— GE, FD, DB, and CA.
A	minor	7th ————	10 semitones.	14, ———— BA, AG, GF, ED, CB.
A	major	7th ————	11 semitones.	15, ———— CB, and FE.
A	perfect	8th, or octave	12 semitones.	16, ———— CC, DD, &c. &c.
A	minor	9th, ————	13 semitones.	17, ———— EF and BC.
A	major	9th, ————	14 semitones.	18, ———— CD, DE, FG, GA, and AB.

---

* The Editor refers for every thing not fully explained in this work, to his Elements of Musical Composition and Rudiments of Playing on the Piano Forte. The latter work contains preludes and modulations which may, it is hoped, be of some use to the extemporaneous performer and young composer. His Rounds for the Piano Forte are intended for the use of persons learning to play from score and clefs.

B

Chromatic intervals are such as cannot be performed upon a diatonic scale without destroying the alphabetical arrangement of the notes.

On the White Keys.

An extreme sharp 2nd is equal to 3 semitones. Ex. 19, such as AB♯, BC𝗑, DE♯, and EF𝗑.

————— flat 3rd ————— 2 ————— 20, AC♭, CE♭♭, DF♭, FA♭♭, or E♯G, and GB♭♭ or F𝗑A.*

————— flat 4th ————— 4 ————— 21, CF♭, FB♭♭, or E♯ A, GC♭.

————— sharp 5th ————— 8 ————— 22, AE♯ or B♭♭F, BF𝗑, or C♭ G and EB♯ or F♭ C.

————— sharp 6th ————— 10 ————— 23, DB♯, EC𝗑, GE♯, AF𝗑 and C♭A.

————— flat 7th ————— 9 ————— 24, CB♭♭, DC♭, E♯D, GF♭.

————— flat 8ve ————— 11 ————— 25, CC♭, or B♯ B♮ and FF♭ or E♯ E♮.

————— sharp 8ve ————— 13 ————— 26, EE♯ or F♭F♮ and BB♯ or C♭ C♮.

————— sharp 9th ————— 15 ————— 27, AB♯ &c. see extreme sharp 2nd.

Enharmonic intervals cannot be distinguished on keyed instruments.—Ex. 29.

A complete knowledge of the major and minor keys is absolutely requisite for the performer from a figured bass; but a long detail of them, and of the manner of forming them, is necessarily avoided in this work; and the Editor again refers the student to his former works already mentioned, and will only insert a list of a few of the major and minor keys, with the number of flats and sharps which characterize them.

		Flats.							Sharps.					
	7	6	5	4	3	2	1	0	1	2	3	4	5	6	7
Major keys.	C♭	G♭	D♭	A♭	E♭	B♭	F	C	G	D	A	E	B	F♯	C♯

		Flats.							Sharps.					
	7	6	5	4	3	2	1	0	1	2	3	4	5	6	7
Minor keys.	A♭	E♭	B♭	F	C	G	D	A	E	B	F♯	C♯	G♯	D♯	A♯

The minor keys are, in music, distinguished from the relative major keys (having a similar number of flats and sharps) by the chromatic alterations which so frequently occur in them.

OF TRIADS.

A triad is a note accompanied by its 3rd and 5th. Thus, the triad of

A is A C and E.
that of B — B D F.
————— C — C E G.
————— D — D F A.
————— E — E G B.
————— F — F A C.
————— G — G B D.

These should be learnt by memory.

Consonant triads have their 5ths perfect.—Ex. 29.

Dissonant triads have their 5ths extreme flat or extreme sharp.—Ex. 30.

Consonant triads are called major triads when their 3rds are major, Ex. 31; and minor triads when their 3rds are minor.—Ex. 32.

In thorough bass, triads occur so frequently, that when they are required to be played, figures are not always put, especially to the first and most accented notes in a bar.

The 8th is added merely to enrich the effect.

---

* An extreme sharp 3rd (5 semitones, as A♭ C♯) occurs in the Adagio of Mozart's Sinfonia, usually called Jupiter. The C♯ is a mere appoggiatura.

RULES FOR PLAYING FROM A FIGURED BASS.

A SUCCESSION OF TRIADS.

When no figures are placed over a bass note, play $\frac{8}{5}\frac{}{3}$ with the right hand on the treble stave, avoiding the extremes of high and low, and placing any one of the three figures at the top, according to circumstances.—Ex. 33. A sharp, natural, or flat, placed over the bass note, as in bars 4, 5, 6, signify that the 3rd is accordingly to be sharp, natural, or flat. The 5th is always perfect when the 3rd is major, unless expressly specified otherwise. The 8th, 5th, or 3rd, without any figures, also stand for $\frac{8}{5}\frac{}{3}$. The 8th is only inserted to make the harmony fuller, and is more frequently omitted than the 5th or 3rd. Indeed the 3rd should not be omitted if possible. The 8th should be omitted in a dissonant triad by the inexperienced performer of thorough bass.—Ex. 34. In playing from a figured bass, the rules of composition must be as strictly observed as in writing music. Hence, two consecutive perfect fifths, or octaves, must not take place between the same parts, as in Ex. 35, 36, 37†. Ex. 38, 39, and 40, are correct, but less convenient than Ex. 44, 45, 46, on account of the unnecessary motion given to the right hand, which should generally remain as still as possible. The upper melody should repeat the same note whenever it can be done; and when that cannot be, should move to the nearest note, excepting when by so doing it produces consecutive fifths or eights. Such transitions, however, as Ex. 38, 39, 40, must occasionally be made to recover the position of the right hand after it has got too low or too high. The same 5th or 8ve repeated, is not considered as a violation of the rule—Ex. 41; nor if one part moves while the other stands still.—Ex. 42. The imperfect 5th will be treated of hereafter. Octaves or unisons may pervade a whole passage. The words " tasto solo" are used to prevent the performer from playing chords when no figures are put—Ex. 43. Octaves may be played below the bass notes without violating the rule—Ex. 44. This is only done to imitate the effect of the double bass in an orchestra, or to increase the loudness. Chords are likewise occasionally played for the same purpose with the left hand and octaves in the right, especially on the harp. But the student is recommended to avoid them for the present. Ex. 44, 45, 46, are respectively preferable for all general purposes to Ex. 38, 39, 40. The student should therefore transpose Ex. 44, 45, 46, into several major and minor keys, both writing them and playing them by memory, placing the chords in all the three positions—Ex. 47 to 60.

Ex. 61 is said to be in the major key of C, because it begins and ends in that key; but it modulates frequently into the relative minor key of A. Where the asterisk is placed (*) in this and in several of the following examples, the less pleasing transition is adopted, generally, for the sake of gaining a good position for the right hand. The student should transpose this into various other major keys, writing only the bass, and playing the chords according to the foregoing rules. Ex. 62 is in A minor, and should likewise be transposed and practised in various other minor keys. Ex. 63, 64, 65, are three different ways of accompanying the same bass, of which the latter is the best, on account of the upper melody having the least motion. See last bar but one of Ex. 62.

OF THE CHORDS OF THE $\frac{6}{3}$ AND $\frac{6}{4}$.

The chord of the 6th is marked $\frac{6}{3}$ or only 6, which stands for $\frac{6}{3}$, because 3 is always understood when 4 or 2 is not expressed. The inexperienced performer will find it safest to perform only two notes with the right hand, the 6th and the 3rd, either of them at the top, according to circumstances, but generally the 6th. The performer who has studied

---

† Some writers have considered contrary motion between the upper melody and the bass as a sufficient rule for the formation of a correct and pleasing accompaniment; but fifths and octaves may occur where there is contrary motion, as in the two last notes of Ex. 35: and the commencement of Ex. 38, 39, and 40, are not so agreeable as that of Ex. 44, 45, 46. See also the Subordinate Rules—Elements of Composition.

composition and can distinguish between such chords of the 6th as are inversions, and such as are not, will, in the latter cases, add an 8th, which he must not do in the former on account of doubling that which was the 3rd note of the triad in its original or direct position—(See Subordinate Rules in the Elements.) Ex. 66 shews the way recommended to the beginner; and Ex. 67 shews how they may be accompanied when known to be inversions, by adding another note in the right hand. Ex. 68 and 69 contain inversions, and should be transposed and practised in various keys. Ex. 70 shews how a succession of ascending or descending 6ths should be accompanied by the beginner. Ex. 71, 72, and 73, shew how another note may be added in the right hand without violating the stricter rules*.

$\frac{6}{4}$ stands for $\frac{8}{6}{4}$. Any one of the 3 notes may be at the top according to circumstances—Ex. 74. Ex. 75 to 80 should

be transposed and practised in all the principal major and minor keys. Ex. 81, being longer, may be transposed into two or three only of the principal keys. Ex. 82 contains illustrations of the four sorts of cadence or termination of passages, the knowledge of which not being essential to the mere performer from a figured bass, a reference is made for the definition of them to the Elements of Composition.

The thorough bass player should always avail himself of the composer's own melody where he has an opportunity, as in chants, psalms, services, and other church music, recitatives, songs, and violin solos. In playing Ex. 83, 84, 85, he must never go above the treble or below the bass, and when these are too near together to admit of a chord between them, he must omit the harmony as in Ex. 85. Given trebles will be found to several other examples in the course of the work.

OF DISCORDS.

We begin (as in the Elements) with discords of addition, and first the dominant 7th, which is a major 3rd, perfect 5th, and minor 7th, to the 5th note of the key, whether major or minor key.

When played full, $\frac{8}{7}{5}{3}$ may be taken in the right hand, any one of the notes at the top—Ex. 86, 88, 90, and 92. The

same chord is transposed into the minor key—Ex. 87, 89, 91, and 93. The discordant note of all discords must fall—here it is the 7th. This note must never be doubled. The leading note of the key should rise; this therefore should not be doubled; the octave stands still. The 3rd and 5th both go to the same note $\begin{smallmatrix}D\\B\end{smallmatrix}\longrightarrow C$ $\begin{smallmatrix}B\\G\sharp\end{smallmatrix}\longrightarrow A$

The dominant 7th, however, should only be occasionally accompanied with four notes in the right hand, as in loud passages; for this accompaniment, together with the bass, constitutes a harmony of five distinct parts; and as one of four parts is considered the most clear and beautiful in composition, so, in playing thorough bass, three notes are generally sufficient in the right hand. The 8th is the least essential note of the dominant 7th, and is most frequently omitted.

7 therefore may stand for $\frac{8}{7}{5}{3}$; but it usually stands for $\frac{7}{5}{3}$.—See Ex. 94 in the major key of C; and 95 in A minor.

The inversions of the dominant 7th are—

The $\frac{6}{5}$ (standing for $\frac{6}{5}{3}$) on the leading note of the key.—Ex. 96, 97

The $\frac{6}{4}{3}$ (sometimes written $\frac{4}{3}$) on the second note of the key.—Ex. 98, 99.

And the $\frac{6}{4}{2}$ (sometimes written $\frac{4}{2}$) on the fourth note of the key.—Ex. 100, 101.

($\frac{4}{2}$ only stands for $\frac{6}{4}{2}$ when the bass note falls to the note below.) Their resolutions will be seen in the above examples.

When the fundamental note of the dominant 7th is altogether omitted, we obtain the dissonant triad—Ex. 102.

---

* A passage of ascending sixes in the minor key is rarely met with.

103, or its inversions, the $\frac{6}{3}$ on the second note of the key—Ex. 104, 105; or the $\frac{6}{4}$ on the 4th note of the key—Ex. 106, 107. The best composers of the antient style of music, and some very eminent modern writers, prefer the $\frac{6}{3}$ on the second note of the key—Ex. 104, 105; to the $\frac{6}{4}$—Ex. 98, 99. On no account therefore should the $\frac{6}{3}$ be supposed to stand for $\frac{6}{4}$. Indeed a fourth is never understood; but always specified in figured basses.

The added 6th is resolved by making the discordant note (viz. the 5th) fall and become the 3rd to the next chord of the fifth of the key.

Ex. 110 and 111 shew the omission of the 3rd.

Ex. 112 and 113 shew the omission of the 5th. The 8th, or bass note, is inserted in the treble, because this 6th is not an inversion of the $\frac{5}{3}$, but the bass note is fundamental and may be doubled.

Ex. 114 and 115 shew the difference between the accompaniment of the $\frac{6}{3}$ to F in the major key of C, where it is not an inversion, and in the minor key of A where it is an inversion. Ex. 116 is the same in the minor key as 114.

The inversions of the $\frac{6}{5}$ on the 4th note of the key, are $\frac{6}{4}$ on the 6th note of the key; $\frac{6}{4}{2}$ on the key note, and $\frac{7}{5}$ on the 2nd note of the key.

Ex. 117 and 118 shew the resolutions of the $\frac{6}{4}$, (sometimes written $\frac{4}{3}$) in the major and minor key. Ex. 119 and 120 shew the $\frac{4}{3}$ with the 6th omitted, a chord not very common in the music of the great masters, as they avoided a perfect 4th to the bass note as much as possible, unless used as a discord of suspension. The $\frac{6}{4}$ without the 3 was still less tolerable, and is therefore omitted in this work. Ex. 121 and 122 shew the resolutions of the $\frac{6}{4}{2}$. Ex. 123 and 124, the $\frac{6}{2}$. Ex. 125 and 126, the $\frac{4}{2}$. $\left(\text{The } \frac{6}{4}{2} \text{ is generally used as a discord of suspension.}\right)$

Ex. 127 and 128 shew the resolution of the $\frac{7}{5}{3}$ on the 2nd note of the key played with four notes in the right hand, the 8th being added for the sake of loudness. Three are in general sufficient—Ex. 129, 130. The $\frac{8}{7}{3}$ or $\frac{8}{7}{5}$ might also be occasionally used, but are omitted as being less agreeable than the $\frac{7}{5}$. Two ways of resolving the $\frac{7}{3}$ are shewn in Ex. 131 and 132. When the 7th is omitted, as in Ex. 133, this chord resembles the triad of the 4th note of the minor key. When transposed into the minor key, Ex. 134, it is not so agreeable to ascend three semitones from F♮ to G♯, as to descend from F to G♯, an extreme flat seventh. Had the F been sharp, it would be better to ascend.—(See Elements of Composition, note on page 51). According to the rules of contrary motion, the student would be induced at first to conclude, that the first way of accompanying the triads, D and G in Ex. 135, was better than the 2nd; but when he reflects, that the fundamental note of this chord is F and not D, (see Ex. 114 and 116), he will perceive that the 2nd method is really agreeable to the laws of contrary motion. The same remarks apply to Ex. 136. (See Elements.) Ex. 137 to 141, are practices for the student who should play them in all keys, transposing Ex. 137, 139, and 141 into other major keys, and 138 and 140 into other minor keys.

Ex. 142 contains various ways in which the added 6th and its inversions may be resolved into the dominant 7th and its inversions; the only rule being that the discordant note (viz. the 5th), must fall. Ex. 143 is the beginning of the same in the minor, which the student must complete. Ex. 144 is merely meant to show, that the added 6th, when the 5th is not retained, may also be succeeded by the dominant 7th: no rule is required.

The added 9th, is a 9th added to the dominant 7th, and the 9th should be placed at the top whenever it is possible; and, at all events, the 3rd should never be placed above the 9th. When the 9th is resolved into the 8th on the same bass note, the 7th, 5th, and 3rd have dashes placed after them, to show that these notes are to be continued, as is the case whenever dashes are put. Ex. 145 and 146 show this resolution of the added 9th. Ex. 147

shows another resolution into the triad of the key note, in which the 5th and 7th must both be resolved into the 3rd note of the next chord, to avoid consecutive perfect 5ths to the upper melody. The same may be done in Ex. 148, though the 5ths are not both perfect: but this resolution is not so agreeable as that into $\begin{smallmatrix}8\\6\\4\end{smallmatrix}$ Ex. 149 and 150. But as three notes are generally better than four in the accompaniment, the 5th of this discord may be omitted. Ex. 151.

So that $\frac{9}{7}$ may be said to stand in general for $\begin{smallmatrix}9\\7\\3\end{smallmatrix}$ or, in full music, for $\begin{smallmatrix}9\\7\\5\\3\end{smallmatrix}$.

The leading 7th, (derived from the added 9th, the fundamental note being omitted), is a 7th on the leading note of the key, whether major, as Ex. 152 and 154, or minor, Ex. 153 and 155. Three positions for the accompaniment are here given, but that in which the 7th is at the top is best. In the minor key this discord is called the diminished 7th, the 3rd being minor, the 5th extreme flat, and the 7th extreme flat. But one inversion of the leading 7th, is found in the major key, (Ex. 156,) in which the 3rd should be at the top, that note being the same which was 7th to the leading note, and 9th in the discord of the added 9th, from which it is derived. In the minor key, however, all the inversions are occasionally met with, and in various positions. Ex. 157.

Ex. 158 is an exercise to be transposed and practised in various other major keys. In the 2nd bar the dissonant triad has an 8ve, as well as a $\begin{smallmatrix}5\\3\end{smallmatrix}$, because the bass is not the 3rd note of the triad from which it is derived. Bars 10, 11, 12, 13, and 15, show how the $\begin{smallmatrix}6\\4\end{smallmatrix}$ on the 5th of the key may be followed by the dominant 7th and its inversions.

The $\begin{smallmatrix}6\\4\end{smallmatrix}$ on the 5th of the key resolved into the $\begin{smallmatrix}5\\3\end{smallmatrix}$ or $\begin{smallmatrix}7\\5\\3\end{smallmatrix}$ is not considered as an inversion of a triad, but as a species of discord, or double appoggiatura. (See Elements.)

Discords of suspension are accented, generally resolved on the same bass note, (as will be specified by the figures of the thorough bass), accompanied by the same notes that usually attend the figure which follows the discord and the discordant note must be always prepared, viz. continued from the same note in the preceding chord or discord. Thus the discord of the 4th is followed by the 3rd on the same bass note, is accompanied by a 5th and 8th, because these notes usually accompany a 3rd, and the discordant note must be continued from the same note in the preceding chord or discord; $\begin{smallmatrix}8\\5\\4\end{smallmatrix}$ is therefore resolved into $\begin{smallmatrix}8\\5\\3\end{smallmatrix}$; $\begin{smallmatrix}8-\\5-\\4\,3.\end{smallmatrix}$ And the 4th must be prepared. $\begin{smallmatrix}5\,-\\4\,\,3\end{smallmatrix}$ or 4 3

stand for $\begin{smallmatrix}8-\\5-\\4\,3\end{smallmatrix}$. No 3 must be played with the 4. See Ex. 159; which also contains the inversion of the same discord, $\begin{smallmatrix}5\\2\end{smallmatrix}$, where the discordant note is in the bass.

Ex. 160 shows the preparation and resolution of the same discord in the minor key, the student being left to vary the position as in Ex. 159.

This discord is sometimes resolved into the dominant 7th. Ex. 161.

A succession of these is sometimes met with, Ex. 162, 163, 164. In Ex. 162 the treble descends so rapidly, that had the first chord in the treble been taken in a position nearer the bass, the two hands would soon have been too close. To avoid this the 5th may ascend to the 8th, while the 4th resolves. Ex. 163 and 164. In the latter, the 4th is supposed to descend to the 3rd in each instance, the parts changing places. Ex. 163, from its clearness, is most agreeable. Ex. 165 and 166 are to be transposed into other major and minor keys, and practised. The $\begin{smallmatrix}7\,6\\4\,-\end{smallmatrix}$ on the 5th of the key, is an inversion of the $\begin{smallmatrix}5\\4\,3\end{smallmatrix}$ seldom met with, excepting in a pedale, or holding note in the bass, as in bar 9 of Ex. 165. Ex. 166, being in triple time, the student must be careful to observe whether the resolution of his discords falls early or late in the bar, viz. whether the 4 is succeeded by the 3 on the 3rd, or on the 2nd note, which he may tell by the situation of the dash, 4—3 or 43—.

The discord of the 9th (not the added 9th) is resolved into an 8th on the same bass note, (and because the 8th ought to be so accompanied) is accompanied with 5 and 3. Thus 9 8 stands for $\begin{smallmatrix}9\,8\\5\,-\\3\,-\end{smallmatrix}$. No 8 must be played with the 9.

The 9 must be prepared from the same note in the preceding chord or discord, (See Ex. 167), which contains most of its resolutions and preparations in the major key, as Ex. 168 does in the minor key. At the end of Ex. 168, the manner in which the 9 is sometimes resolved into a 3 or a 6 on another bass note may be seen. Ex. 169 shews how the 9 8 and 4 3 may be used on alternate bass notes.—On an organ the ligatured or tied notes should be held down; on a pianoforte they may be struck or repeated *. In the latter half of this example the 1st and 2nd parts are supposed to cross each other, as is specified by the words 2nd part, 1st part, &c. Ex. 170 shows the same passage in another position, less favourable for execution, and less agreeable in its upper melody than the former. Ex. 171 is still more difficult of execution and less fit for thorough bass. Ex. 169 therefore alone need be transposed and practised.

The discord of the 7 (not the dominant or added 7th, nor that which is an inversion of the added 6th, nor yet any which will hereafter be described) may be resolved into a 6th on the same bass note; and (as the 6th is so accompanied) should be accompanied only with a 3rd, and occasionally with an 8th; but not (in general) with a 5th.

7 6, therefore, stands for $\begin{smallmatrix}7&6\\3&\_\end{smallmatrix}$. The 7 must be prepared from the same note in the preceding chord. The 3rd, therefore, may sometimes be over the 7: but as a succession of 6ths sounds best with the 6th at the stop (Ex. 70 to 75); and as the 7th is only a species of appoggiatura, as the 5 is to the 6th, in ascending, Ex. 172, it is better that the 7 and 5 should be at the top when followed by a 6: hence 5 6 stands for $\begin{smallmatrix}5&6\\3&\_\end{smallmatrix}$; but no 8th, especially when there is a succession of them.

The 7 6 in the cadences Ex. 173 is sometimes accompanied as in Ex. 174; but in this case the writer of the thorough bass should express it in the figures Ex. 175, and the performer must be careful to remove the 5th when he plays the 6th.

The $\begin{smallmatrix}7\\5\\3\end{smallmatrix}$ on the fourth note of the key is peculiar to ancient music. It is generally resolved into the added 6 or $\begin{smallmatrix}6\\5\\3\end{smallmatrix}$; the 5th, or 5th and 3rd, being expressed in the figures, Ex. 176 and 177. Ex. 178 shows how discords of addition may be prepared, or used as discords of suspension.

Ex. 179 shows what a variety of figures may be used as discords of suspension on a pedale or holding note in the bass. The performer of thorough bass is recommended not to insert any additional note not expressed in the figures, which he might imagine would complete the harmony, as he cannot always be certain of the composer's intentions.

Hence $\begin{smallmatrix}6&\_\\5&4\end{smallmatrix}$ on the same bass note must not have a third added, but is an exception to a general rule. Hence also, $\begin{smallmatrix}8&\_\\7&6\end{smallmatrix}$; indeed, $\begin{smallmatrix}8\\6\end{smallmatrix}$ should never have an additional note given to it. The 4th is sometimes understood, but the effect is not generally improved by its insertion.

Many passages of great simplicity, when accompanying their usual basses, are rendered extremely difficult by being reckoned from a pedale or holding note, usually on the 5th of the key, or sometimes on the key note, as in Ex. 180. The 4 3 is sometimes found with the dominant 7th and the added 9th. Ex. 181.

Two or more notes prepared and resolved together are called double discords. Ex. 182, 184, and 185. The discords of the $\begin{smallmatrix}7&8\\5&\_\\4\\2&3\end{smallmatrix}$ on the key note may be written $\begin{smallmatrix}9&8\\7\\5&\_\\4&3\end{smallmatrix}$. Ex. 183.

When the major or sharp 7th on the key note is followed by an 8ve, it is always understood to mean the above discord, and should be accompanied with $\begin{smallmatrix}2\\4\end{smallmatrix}$ or $\begin{smallmatrix}5\\4\\2\end{smallmatrix}$. Ex. 186.

Ex. 187 and 188 must be transposed and practised in various keys. Wherever the asterisk (*) is put, the treble hand ascends, on account of the tendency which melody, (especially when replete with discords), has to descend. The omission of the 5th at the end of bar 3rd, and of the 8th at the beginning of bar the 4th (Ex. 137), is immaterial.

---

* The Editor having mentioned this quality of protracting or sustaining sounds, so characteristic of the organ, cannot resist the opportunity it affords him, of entering his protest against the abuse of this noble instrument, so frequent among organists, who, because it may well be denominated a " vocal frame," on which they may add " length to solemn sounds," will never suffer you to have a short note, a rest, a pause, or a passage that is mezzo staccato, or that has any animation, or resemblance to the effect which the same passage would have performed elsewhere. Let the chant, the service, the anthem, the psalm, the organ fugue, &c. be played in the genuine organ style; but, if a spirited chorus or overture be adopted as a voluntary, let the performer imitate the effect it would have in a full band, and not reduce its brilliancy into an unvaried drawl.

In bar the 9th, the 5th is inserted with the dominant 7th to prepare the next discord; and this constitutes a most difficult part of thorough bass. In bar 13 the parts are supposed to change places, the 7th of the first discord falling, and the 5th rising to the 3rd of the next discord. In bar 15 the added 6th is accompanied with an 8th, to prepare the next discord. The last chord of bar 4, Ex. 188, has an 8th added to prepare the next discord. At the end of bar 5 a 3rd is inserted, as this note should not be omitted.

Discords of transition consist of notes not belonging to the preceding chord (whether discordant notes or not), passing diatonically up or down the scale while some note is held. They are accompanied the same as the preceding note from which they pass. Thus a 7 following an 8 on the same bass note (Ex. 189 is accompanied with the $\frac{5}{3}$ which belonged to the 8, and the 7 must fall to the note below in the next chord, because it is a descending passing note.

Hence 8 7 stands for $\frac{8\ 7}{5\ -}{3\ -}$; but it will not be always practicable to insert both the 5th and the 3rd, on account of the stricter rules.

The 5 following a 6 may be accompanied by a 3, or a 6 and 3. The 5 is a descending passing note. Ex. 190. At the end of bar 1 2 3 the bass note is the passing note, and is sometimes figured $4, \frac{6}{2}\frac{4}{2}$, or 2, or merely with dashes, as in bar 2 and 3.

A 6 following a 5 is an ascending passing note. The 4 following a 3 is the same. Ex. 191. In Ex. 192 the nature of ascending and descending passing notes is shown, while the whole triad, or part of it, is held by other parts. These, in thorough bass, produce a variety of figures; but the use of dashes will render the performance easier. The principal discords of transition are the $\frac{4}{2}$ and its inversions the $\frac{7}{3}$ and $\frac{6}{5}$.

$\frac{4}{2}$ preceded and followed by $\frac{5}{3}$ on the same bass note, must not be accompanied by a 6th, (as in Ex. 121 and 122.) Ex. 193; but it may occasionally have a 5 or an 8, as in Ex. 194.

Ex. 195 and 196 are inversions of the $\frac{4}{2}$, and the superiority of the dash, where it can be used instead of new figures, for the repetition of the same note, will be readily perceived. In 197 and 200, the discords, or passing notes, are in the bass.

In Ex. 198 and 199, the manner of adding a third part in the accompaniment may be seen.

Under the head of discords of transition may also be classed a succession of sixes on a pedale, descending, or ascending. Ex. 200. Also discords of addition on a pedale unprepared (Ex. 202), in which the manner proposed by some writers, of figuring the dominant 7th, added 9th, and leading 7th, on a pedale, is shown. In playing the $\frac{7}{6}{4}$ and the $\frac{7}{6}{4}{2}$ on the key note, the 6th note should always be placed in the upper melody. Ex. 203 is to be transposed and practised.

Discords of syncopation are successions of 7ths on each note (Ex. 204), or on the alternate notes (Ex. 205) of a bass, which continually falls 5ths, or rises 4ths, or does so alternately. They may be accompanied with $\frac{8}{5}{3}$ (Ex. 204 and 205), for fulness, or with only $\frac{5}{3}$ or $\frac{8}{3}$. The discordant notes must all be prepared like discords of suspension, and resolved by falling to the note below in the next chord.

There are no inversions of a succession of 7ths on each bass note: but there are two inversions of 7ths on alternate bass notes. Ex. 206 and 207. Ex. 208 must be transposed and practised as usual.

Chromatic harmony consists of chords, in which the alteration of flats and sharps does not change the key. Ex. 209 consists of chromatic passing notes, ascending and descending. Ex. 210, 211, 212, and 213, are discords of transition rendered chromatic. Ex. 211. The extreme flat 3rd to the 4th note of the key sharpened (called Fa sharp in the Elements) was, the last adopted, because, perhaps, the least agreeable.

The foregoing examples (209 to 213) are in the major key of C; and they cannot all be transposed into the minor. Ex. 214 contains the principal. Ex. 215 is the minor 9th introduced into the major key of C; also the diminished 7th and one of its inversions. Ex. 216 shews how the 4th of the key, sharpened, (fa sharp), may be accompanied and resolved in the major key of C. In Ex. 217, the 3rd to this chromatic note, in the minor key must be sharpened. The student may transpose the rest of Ex. 216 into the minor key of A. Ex. 218 shows how some writers used the 6th sharpened on this bass note, instead of the 7th flattened, as in Ex. 216. This can only be done when the 6th ascends. It cannot be transposed into the minor key, as the 2nd note of the minor key cannot be made extreme sharp.

The extreme sharp 6th in the minor key is occasioned by the 4th of the key being sharpened when it is in the accompaniment. It is called the Italian 6th, when accompanied only by a 3rd, (see Ex. 219). In the minor key of A, (Ex. 220); in the major key of C, in which the bass is flattened, as well as the treble sharpened, or they would not constitute an extreme sharp 6th. The extreme sharp 6th, when accompanied by a 5th as well as a 3rd, is called the German 6th. Ex. 221, in the minor key of A, and Ex. 222, in the major key of C. This discord should not be resolved into a $\frac{5}{3}$, but into a $\frac{6}{4}$, to avoid consecutive 5ths. When accompanied with a $\frac{4}{3}$ the extreme sharp 6th is called the French 6th. Ex. 223, 224. The Neapolitan 6th in the minor key is simply the 6th to the fourth note of the key, flattened, and should generally be placed at the top. Ex. 225. In the major key, the 3rd as well as the 6th is flattened, so that this chord is the same in both keys. Ex. 226. A passage peculiar to church music may be seen, Ex. 227, 228. A flat 7th to the key note not followed by any other alterations of the flats and sharps, may be considered as a chromatic licence. Ex. 229. Of the same nature seems to be the second bass note of Ex. 230. The student should transpose and practise Ex. 231, 232; the former, in the minor key, is put first, as being most simple. The upper notes are given, and some of the chords; but in transposing them they may be left out.

For the study of the unessential notes of melody, the composition of music in parts, and the various kinds of time, the reader is unavoidably referred to the Elements of Composition. Modulation is also, indeed, as much a peculiar branch of composition as they are; and the thorough bass player, finding the modulations already made for him is not under the necessity of understanding them: but as it is hoped that the playing thorough bass will not generally be separated, as hitherto, from a knowledge of composition, we shall proceed to offer some examples of what is contained in the work already referred to, on this subject.

Diatonic modulation changes the key from the major to the relative minor, and the reverse, without any alteration of flats and sharps; Ex. 233. Chromatic modulation is a change of key, together with an alteration of the flats and sharps, as in all the following examples of modulation. Natural modulation is when the keys, into which the changes are made, are those most immediately related to the original key, viz. the dominant key, the subdominant, the relative, its dominant, and its subdominant; or, in other words, keys that have the same number of flats or sharps, or only one flat or sharp more or less than the original key has. Thus, from C major the natural modulations are into G major, F major, A minor, E minor, and D minor; and from G minor into D minor, C minor, B♭ major, F major, and E♭ major. Modulations from C major into D major, B♭ major, C minor, &c. would be unnatural or extraneous, and produce a more unexpected effect. Gradual modulation is effected by doubtful chords, viz. by such as belong to both keys, and therefore render the transition imperceptible, as from C to G, Ex. 235, where the first triad of the second bar belongs to both C and G. (Similar modulations to this, as from F to C, may be made by transposition). From G to C, (Ex. 236), where the middle triad of the second bar is the doubtful chord. In modulating from F to G and from G to F, if C major or A minor is the original key, the modulation is natural, but if G or F, major, or E or D minor, are the original keys, the modulation is unnatural. In Ex. 237, 238, the modulation is gradual, the triad, common to both keys, being that of C. In passing to the relative minor, or the reverse, the doubtful chords may be the added 6th, (the 5th being omitted), the dissonant triad, and the leading 7th, Ex. 239 to 243. In Ex. 244, the Neapolitan 6th, and other discords, are common to both keys; some of the modulations are natural and others extraneous. Ex. 245 is a specimen of natural and gradual modulation, though various discords are used. Ex. 246 is a specimen of natural, but sudden modulation, the precise moment of the change of key being perceptible. For the order and duration of modulations, see Elements, page 89. Ex. 247 shows the manner of modulating by a succession of discords of syncopation. Ex. 248 is a modulation by dominant 7ths, in succession. Ex. 249 is modulation by diminished 7ths, alternately inverted on a bass of descending semitones. Ex. 250 is the same on an ascending bass, and is of more modern invention.

Enharmonic modulation is the adoption of some other note in a chord, which, on a keyed instrument, sounds the same as one we have, or might have, as by taking E♯, where we have, or might have, F♮, &c. The first chord in each bar of Ex. 251 and 252 sounds the same on a piano forte, viz.

A♭	G♯	G♯	A♭
F	F	E♯	F
D	D	D	D
B	B	B	C♭

In Ex. 251 these are resolved into four minor and four major keys; and Ex. 252 into four other minor and major keys. The Italian and German 6ths may be used in enharmonic modulations. Ex. 253, 254. All the examples, from 233 to 254, should be transposed and practised. Ex. 291 also contains enharmonic modulations.

OF ACCOMPANYING THE SCALE.

As the thorough bass player is sometimes expected to play an accompaniment to the major and minor scales, ascending and descending, in the bass or treble, he will find one of each, Ex. 255 and 256. Those which are generally taught contain modulations, and are sometimes incorrect. But the chief objection to them is that they are generally given him to perform by rote, before he has learnt the meaning either of discords or modulation; and what the utility of this can be, the author is unable to inform his reader. There is in fact no accompaniment peculiar to such a scale. Ex. 257 and 258 contain several varieties, which might be very considerably augmented.

A SHORT RECAPITULATION OF THE RULES RELATING TO THE CHORDS AND DISCORDS MOST FREQUENTLY USED.

When no figures are put, play $\frac{8}{5}$.
$$\frac{3}{}$$

8, 5, or 3, with no other figures, stands for $\begin{smallmatrix}8\\5\\3\end{smallmatrix}$.

In a dissonant triad add no 8 in general, especially if it doubles the 3rd note of the chord from which it is derived.

A ♯, ♭, or ♮, (not placed against a figure, but under them, or by themselves), shows that the 3rd is accordingly to be made ♯, ♭, or ♮. In old music, ♭ means a minor 3rd, and ♯ a major.

When the 3rd is major, the 5th must always be made perfect, unless the contrary is specified.

In playing a succession of triads, avoid consecutive perfect 5ths and 8ves between any two of the parts.

Make the upper part stand still, if the same note occurs in the next triad; if not, make it move as little as possible. Exceptions may be made to this rule, when the right hand is too high or too low.

6 stands for $\begin{smallmatrix}6\\3\end{smallmatrix}$. When this chord is the inversion of a triad, the 3rd or the 6th may be doubled. But the 8ve should only be added when it does not double the 3rd note of the triad from which it is derived. It is generally best, and especially in a succession of 6ths, to place the 6th note at the top.

A ♯, ♮, or ♭, before any figure, makes it, accordingly, ♯, ♮, or ♭, as ♯ 2, ♯ 3, ♯4, ♭5, &c,: but 6, 4, or 5, with a line drawn through them, stand also for a sharpened 6th and 4th. Amongst flats this mark makes the 6th or 4th natural. If already sharp, it would make them double sharp. The ♭ in old music is used to contradict the ♯, and is then equivalent to our ♮. 5, with a line drawn through it, is used by some writers for the extreme flat 5th.

$\begin{smallmatrix}6\\4\end{smallmatrix}$ stands for $\begin{smallmatrix}8\\6\\4\end{smallmatrix}$, except in the inversions of the dissonant triad, when the 8th is better omitted.

When $\begin{smallmatrix}6\\4\end{smallmatrix}$ is followed by $\begin{smallmatrix}5\\3\end{smallmatrix}$ on the same bass note, always make 6 go to 5, and 4 to 3.

7 stands for $\begin{smallmatrix}7\\3\\5\end{smallmatrix}$; or, in full passages, for $\begin{smallmatrix}8\\7\\5\\3\end{smallmatrix}$.

The discordant note in all discords, (excepting some of transition), must fall.

$\begin{smallmatrix}6\\5\end{smallmatrix}$ stands for $\begin{smallmatrix}6\\5\\3\end{smallmatrix}$, a 3rd being always understood with any figure, where 4 or 2 is not expressed. An exception to this is the $\begin{smallmatrix}6\\5\end{smallmatrix}$ followed by $\begin{smallmatrix}6\\4\end{smallmatrix}$ on the same bass note, which must have no 3.

$\frac{4}{3}$ stands for $\begin{smallmatrix}6\\4\\3\end{smallmatrix}$

$\frac{4}{2}$ stands for $\begin{smallmatrix}6\\4\\2\end{smallmatrix}$ when the bass note falls afterwards one note: but on a pedale or holding note in the bass, $\frac{4}{2}$ must have no 6th, but rather an 8 or 5.

$\frac{9}{7}$ stands for $\begin{smallmatrix}9\\7\\5\\3\end{smallmatrix}$ or for $\begin{smallmatrix}9\\7\\3\end{smallmatrix}$. The 9th should always be placed at the top:—hence

In the leading 7th, the 7th should always be at the top. And

In the $\begin{smallmatrix}6\\4\\3\end{smallmatrix}$ on the 4th note of the key, the 3rd should always be at the top.

A dash (—) placed after a figure, shows the retention or repetition of the note represented by the preceding figure. $\begin{smallmatrix}6&—\\5&4\end{smallmatrix}$ means $\begin{smallmatrix}6&6\\5&4\end{smallmatrix}$. When the composer uses no dashes, the performer must understand them as well as he can.

All discords of suspension must be prepared.

4 3 and $\begin{smallmatrix}5&—\\4&3\end{smallmatrix}$ stands for $\begin{smallmatrix}8&—\\5&—\\4&3\end{smallmatrix}$

$\frac{5}{2}$ may have the 5 or the 2 doubled, but must not have an 8.

9 8 stands for $\begin{smallmatrix}9&8\\5&—\\3&—\end{smallmatrix}$

7 6 stands for $\begin{smallmatrix}7&6\\3&—\end{smallmatrix}$

$\frac{5}{6}$ stands for $\begin{smallmatrix}5&6\\3&—\end{smallmatrix}$

$\begin{smallmatrix}7&6\\5&—\end{smallmatrix}$ stands for $\begin{smallmatrix}7&6\\5&—\\3&—\end{smallmatrix}$

$\begin{smallmatrix}7&6\\5&3\end{smallmatrix}$ must have no 5 with the 6.

$\begin{smallmatrix}8&—\\7&6\end{smallmatrix}$ $\begin{smallmatrix}7&—\\6&5\end{smallmatrix}$ $\begin{smallmatrix}6&—\\5&4\end{smallmatrix}$, &c. may have an 8th added.

$\frac{8}{6}$ should have no note added, except the 8th.

7 8 on the key note stands for $\begin{smallmatrix}7&8\\4&\\2&3\end{smallmatrix}$ or $\begin{smallmatrix}7&8\\5&—\\4&\\2&3\end{smallmatrix}$ and is sometimes written $\begin{smallmatrix}9&8\\4&3\end{smallmatrix}$ or $\begin{smallmatrix}9&8\\5&—\\4&3\end{smallmatrix}$

8 7 stands for $\begin{smallmatrix}8&7\\5&—\\3&—\end{smallmatrix}$

$\begin{smallmatrix}7\\6\\4\end{smallmatrix}$ or $\begin{smallmatrix}7\\6\\4\\2\end{smallmatrix}$ or $\begin{smallmatrix}7\\6\\5\\4\\2\end{smallmatrix}$ on a holding key note, should have the 6th note at the top. This discord has been written $\begin{smallmatrix}13\\11\\9\\7\\5\end{smallmatrix}$

The student may now encounter the difficulties of thorough bass contained in the selection which follows of the music of various ages and different styles. These difficulties are occasioned by the circumstance of figures having been originally intended merely as hints to experienced professors presiding in the orchestras of the oratorio, opera, or concert, and not as a perfect substitution for notes to be performed equally by those who have or have not studied composition.

In the choice of position he will find much difficulty, as it is not possible to play some passages in more than one position, without making consecutive fifths or octaves.

The preparation of suspended discords is likewise difficult.

The utility of the dash must have been obvious from the foregoing examples: but as all writers do not use this sign, the student must endeavour to do without it as much as possible, and may therefore leave it out in his transpositions:

for even those writers who have adopted this mark to slow bass notes, omit it to those which are rapid. Thus, in Ex. 274, bar 3 must be played like bar 1, and bar 6 like bar 5.

Many difficulties arise from inaccuracy, some from inconsistency, and others from the invention being in its infancy, when the best methods of writing figures were not known. By comparing the bass part of Corelli's Concertos with Dr. Pepusch's score, a difference in the manner of figuring the same passages will often be found, as in Ex. 275, the fourth Concerto.

When the same bass note is repeated, the same accompaniment is to be understood. The student must not imagine any changes of chord or key that he does not see expressed, or may infer from the bass itself. In short, if the performer fancies a dash over every note where there are no figures, excepting the first note and the principal accented notes in each bar, he will find the whole tolerably easy. In the first bar of the 2nd part of the vivace, the ♭ 5 means that the ♮ is to be flattened, or made natural, and so of the ♭ 4 in the next bar: but this method is now obsolete. The last note in bars 9 and 10, are to be like the 1st. In bars 9 and 11 of the 2nd part of the allegro, the 3rd to E ♮ must be G ♯, though not specified, as also in bars 15, 16, 18, 20.

The 8th Concerto of Corelli (Ex. 276) is figured from the score; and here, instead of ♯ 6 and ♯ 4, we find 6 and 4 with lines drawn through them. Still a flat signifies a natural, where it is put to contradict a sharp. The principal key of the piece is G minor, but only one flat is placed at the beginning of the stave. So the 2nd Concerto in C minor has only two flats. The 5th and 11th in B♭ major have but one flat. In Handel's earlier productions, three sharps or flats were put when four were required; and the last movement of the Concerto before us is in the key of G major, though no sharp is put at the beginning of the stave. The 5th bar of the first movement is to be played as in Ex. 277. In bar 11 of the movement marked grave, the sharp over D implies that the 5th A must be natural, though there was A♭ put before. In the next two adagios, the figures placed over the semiquaver rests must be reckoned from the following notes. Bar 9, in the 2nd of these adagios, would have been easier to read if written as in Ex. 278. In the vivace, dashes must be understood to all but the first notes of each bar.

Near the conclusion of the allegro, two bars, having no figures at the beginning of line 2, page 31, may be played as in Ex. 279. In the pastorale, the 5th and 6th bars may be played as in Ex. 280; as also in similar places. The succession of 7 6 bar 14, &c. is to be played as in Ex. 281. A dash between the 7 and the 6 would have made it clearer. Ex. 282 and 283 are from Corelli's Trios or Sonatas, for two violins and violoncello. His Sonatas for the violin are better known by the name of Solos. In accompanying the latter, as the performer has an opportunity of availing himself of the composer's melody, where he plays from the original work, he will take it in general (when it does not go too high) as a given melody. In Ex. 284 the violin part is inserted with such an accompaniment as the Editor recommends. In Ex. 285 and 286, the figures over the rests are reckoned from the preceding notes. In accompanying recitatives or songs, the upper note of the harmony should be made to coincide with the voice part as much as possible, as it not only assists the singer, but avoids consecutive octaves. In Ex. 287, (the song usually called Mad Bess, by Purcell), this is elucidated. The thorough bass is frequently omitted in Purcell's music. Ex. 288 shows the style of recitative in Handel's time; and it has not received much alteration since. Bar 4 is to be played as in Ex. 289, and the last bar as in Ex. 290, and so in all similar places. The time of a recitative is not strict, but all ad libitum for the singer. The performer must be guided in striking the chords, by the arrival of the voice at the corresponding note in the melody. Some persons hold the chords, some play them arpeggio, and some make them staccato even when marked to be held; and each of these methods is occasionally good, the object of the performer being ever to assist, but not overpower the singer. Ex. 291 is given as a specimen of enharmonic modulation from Handel. Ex. 292 is an ingenious and elaborate harmony on a ground bass, by Sebastian Bach. Ex. 293 is a beautiful chorus in Iphigenie by Gluck, Ex. 294, is the concluding part of a slow movement, from a Sinfonia, by Haydn, the treble of which is given as a fine specimen of double counterpoint, or two parts changing places with each other, as is the case with the violins and basses in the theme, and all the variations which precede this fragment.

Lastly, the student is recommended, while performing the above selection from classical works arranged in chronological order, to observe the gradual increase of the various discords and modulations, and the application of them to different styles and effects. Let him notice the simple sublimity of the church style, the chaste beauty of the madrigal, and the varied expression of the cantata, with the invention of the ornamental style, so appropriate to instrumental music. By thus arranging his ideas, he will form his taste, and learn to appreciate real excellence of various kinds, without expecting or wishing to see these styles confounded, as they too often are by composers of the present day, who improve church music and madrigals on the same principles that the ecclesiastics of earlier times improved our Gothic cathedrals, by adding screens, stalls, and altar pieces of Grecian architecture. The taste of this nation has acknowledged, and is quickly remedying these barbarities. Let then our lovers of music also endeavour to understand the characteristic merits of each style. So we may hope that our composers will not be tempted to follow the example of the continent, in mingling sacred, secular, vocal, and instrumental music into one incongruous whole.

FINIS.

Mallett, Printer, 59, Wardour Street, Soho.

Ex: 1.
7 Semitones
Ex: 2.
DIATONIC SCALES.
Ex: 3.
&c.
&c.
&c.
7 Semitones
1 Semitone each.
DIATONIC INTERVALS.
Ex: 4.
Minor 2nds
Ex: 5.
Major 2nds
Ex: 6.
Minor 3rds
Ex: 7.
Major 3rds
Ex: 8.
Perfect 4ths
Ex: 9.
Extreme Sharp 4ths
Ex: 10.
Extreme Flat 5ths
Ex: 11.
Perfect 5ths
Ex: 12.
Minor 6ths
Ex: 13.
Major 6ths
Ex: 14.
Minor 7ths
Ex: 15.
Major 7ths
Ex: 16.
Octaves
Ex: 17.
Minor 9ths
Ex: 18.
Major 9ths

CHROMATIC INTERVALS.

Ex: 44.   Ex: 45.   Ex: 46.   Ex: 47.   Ex: 48.   Ex: 49.
C. Major.   G. Major.   D. Major.   A. Major.
Ex: 50.   Ex: 51.   Ex: 52.   Ex: 53.   Ex: 54.
E. Major.   F. Major.   B♭. Major.   E♭. Major.   A. Minor.
Ex: 55.   Ex: 56.   Ex: 57.   Ex: 58.   Ex: 59.   Ex: 60.
E. Minor.   B. Minor.   F♯. Minor.   D. Minor.   G. Minor.   C. Minor.
Ex: 61.
Ex: 62.
Ex: 63.   Ex: 64.   Ex: 65.   Ex: 66.   Ex: 67.

Ex: 68.
Ex 69.
Ex: 70.
Ex: 71.
Ex: 72.
Ex: 73.
Ex: 74.
Ex: 75.
Ex: 76.
Ex: 77.
Ex: 78.
Ex: 79.
Ex: 80.
Ex 81.
Ex: 82.
Close
half close
close
close
close delayed
close
close
half close
close
half close
deceptive close
close
Ex: 83.
Tallis 1510
Ex: 84.
W. Vicary Mus: B. Oxon.

Discords of Addition.

Ex: 85.
Ex: 86. Ex: 87. Ex: 88. Ex: 89. Ex: 90. Ex: 91. Ex: 92. Ex: 93.
Ex: 94. Ex: 95. Ex: 96. Ex: 97. Ex: 98.
Ex: 99. Ex: 100. Ex: 101. Ex: 102. Ex: 103.
Ex: 104. Ex: 105. Ex: 106. Ex: 107.
Ex: 108. Ex: 109. Ex: 110. Ex: 111. Ex: 112.
Ex: 113. Ex: 114. Ex: 115. Ex: 116. Ex: 117. Ex: 118.
or thus
or thus
or thus
or thus

Ex: 119.
Ex: 120.
Ex: 121.
Ex: 122.
Ex: 123.
Ex: 124.
Ex: 125.
Ex: 126.
Ex: 127.
Ex: 128.
Ex: 129.
Ex: 130.
Ex: 131.
Ex: 132.
Ex: 133.
Ex: 134.
or thus
or better thus
or thus
Ex: 135.
Ex: 136.
or better thus
Or better thus
Ex: 137.
Ex: 138.
Ex: 139.
Ex: 140.
Ex: 141.
Ex: 142.

Ex: 143.
Ex: 144.
Ex:145. Ex:146. Ex:147.   Ex:148. Ex:149. Ex:150.   Ex:151.
Ex: 152.
Ex: 153.
Ex: 154. Ex:155. Ex:156. Ex:157.
Ex:158.
Ex: 159   Discords of Suspension.
2073

Ex: 160

Ex: 161.
Ex: 162.
Ex: 163.
Ex: 164.
Ex: 165.
Ex: 166.
Ex: 167.
Ex: 168.

Ex: 169.
2d Part. 1st Part. 2d   1st   &c.
Ex: 170.
Ex: 171.
Ex: 172
Ex: 173.
Ex: 174.
Ex: 175.

Ex: 176.
Ex: 177.
Ex: 178.
Ex: 179.
2d Part. 1st Part. 2d
Ex: 180.
Ex: 181.
Ex: 182.
Ex: 183.

Ex: 184.
Ex: 185.
Ex: 186.
Ex: 187.
Ex: 188.
2073

Discords of Transition.
Ex: 189.

Ex: 199.
Ex: 200.
Ex: 201.
Ex: 202.
Thus figured
by some writers
Ex: 203.
Ex: 204. Discords of Syncopation.
Or thus
&c.

Ex: 205.
Ex: 206.
Ex: 207. 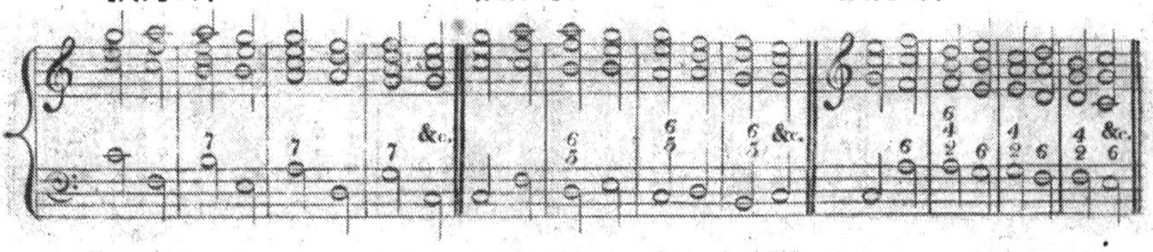
Ex: 208. 
Ex: 209. Chromatic Discords & Harmonies. 
Ex: 210.
2078

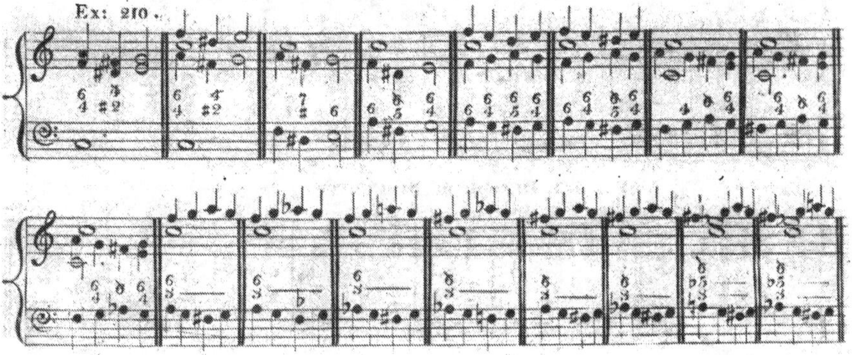

Ex: 211. Ex: 212.
Ex: 213. Ex: 214.
Ex: 215.
Ex: 216.
Ex: 217.
Ex: 218.
Ex: 219.
Ex: 220.
Ex: 221.
Ex: 222.
Ex: 223.

Ex: 224.
Ex: 225
Ex: 226.
Ex: 227.
Ex: 228.
Ex: 229.
Ex: 230.
Ex: 231.
Ex: 232.

Ex: 233. Modulation.
C. Maj: A. Min: C. Maj: A. Min: C. Maj: A. Min: C. Maj:
Ex: 234.
C. Maj: A. Min:
C. Maj: A. Min:
Ex: 235. C to G. Maj:
Ex: 236. G to C.
C. Maj:
Ex: 237. F. to G.
Ex: 238. G to F.
Ex: 239. C. to A. Min:
Ex: 240. A. Min: to C Maj:
Ex: 241. C to A Min:
Ex: 242. A Min: to C Maj:
Ex: 243. C Maj: to A Min: & back to C
Ex: 244.
C. Maj:
E. Min:
C. Maj:
A. Min:
C. Maj
F. Maj:
C. Maj:
F. Maj:
F. Min:
C. Maj:
C. Min:
G. Min:
G. Maj:
C. Maj:
C. Min:
C. Maj:
Ab Maj:
Ex: 245.
C. Min:
C. Maj:
C
G
A. Min:
D. Min:

Ex: 246.
F. Maj: C.Maj   C   G.   A. Min: D. Min: G.Maj: E. Min:
Ex: 247.
C. Maj: in C   C to F   E. Min:
Ex: 248.
C.Maj: F.Maj: C to F.   E. Min: A D G C
Ex: 249.   Ex: 250.   Ex: 251.
C to F.   C   F
Ex: 252.
Ex: 253.   Ex: 254.
Ex: 255. Accompaniments of the Scale.
Ex: 256.

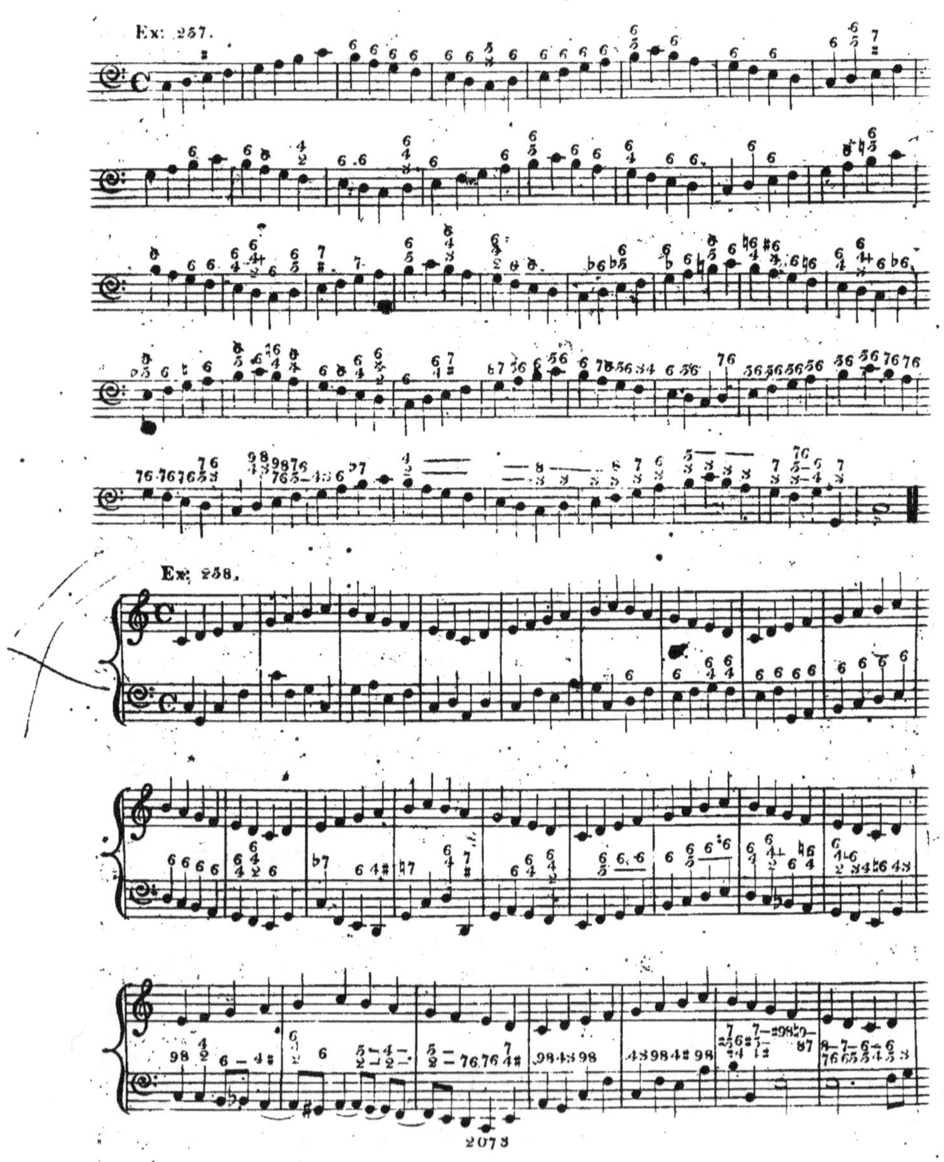
Ex: 257.
Ex: 258.
2073

Ex: 259.
Ps: 1st
Selection of Pieces for Practice.
Martin Luther 1520.
2073
V. S

Ex: 260.
Ps: 38.
Ex: 261.
Gloria Patri to the Nunc Dimittis
Ferrari 16th Century
Ex: 262.
Chorus from the earliest Oratorio known.
Emilie dal Cavaliere. Printed 1600
Ex: 263.
Madrigal the Silver Swan.
Orlando Gibbons early part of the 17. Century
Slow.

Ex: 264.
Madrigal. Awake Sweet love.
John Dowland.
Slow.
Ex: 265.
Motett for the festival of St Peter & St Paul.
Carissimi. Middle of the 17th Century.
Slow.
Ex: 266.
Cho: Et Ululantes.
Carissimi.
Ex: 267.
Cho: Abiit ergo in montes.
Carissimi.

Ex: 268.
Cho: "Plorate Filiae"
Carissimi.
Tasto
Slow
Ex: 269.
Part of a Cantata. Non dar piu pene.
Alessᵒ Scarlatti. latter part of the 17. Century.
fine
Tasto Solo
D.C. al Segno
Ex: 270.
Aria. Il mio figlio d'ovè
Alᵒ Scarlatti
Slow.   Tasto Solo

Ex: 271.
Part of a Cantata "Che mesta"
Al.° Scarlatti.
Slow.
Full Anthem "Teach me O Lord"
Ex: 272.
Rogers
Slow.
Part of a Cantata "Crine Vezzose" in the Ch: Ch: Library.
Ex: 273.
Supposed to be Al.° Scarlatti.
Slow.

Ex: 274.
Part of a Cantata "Taci O Cruda".
Allegro Moderato.
Ex: 275.
Concerto 4th.
Allegro.
Corelli
Adagio
Concerto 4th.

2073

Adagio.
Vivace.
Allegro.
2073.

Vivace
Ex: 276.
Concerto 8th
Vivace.
Grave.
Corelli.
Allegro.

Adagio
Allegro
2073

Adagio.
Vivace.
Allegro.

Pastorale.
1st
2d
12
8

Ex: 277.
Ex: 278.
Ex: 279.
Ex: 280.
Ex: 281.
Ex: 282.
Part of the Second Sonata or Trio Op: I.
Corelli.
Grave.
Vivace.
2073

Ex: 283.
Fugue from the 4th Sonata. Op: 3.   Corelli.

2079

Ex: 286.
Corelli.
The Ninth Solo.
Largo.
Allegro Giga.

Adagio.
Allegro.
D.C.

Ex: 287.
Song "Bess of Bedlam"
H. Purcell early part of the 18th. Century.
Recit: Ad Lib:
From silent shades and the Elysian groves where sad departed
Arp? Ad Lib:
spirits mourn their loves From chrystal streams and from that country
where Jove crowns the fields with flowers all the year Poor senseless
Bess cloth'd in her rags and folly Is come to cure her love-sick melancholy
2073

VIVACE.
Bright Cynthia kept her revels late While Mab the fairy queen did dance And O be...
...ron did sit in state While Mars at Ve...nus hurl'd his lance In yon...der cow...slip
LENTO.
lies my dear Entomb'd in li...quid gems of dew Each day I'll wa...ter it
with a tear Its fading blossom to re.... new For since my love is dead and all my joys are
RECIT:

MODERATO.
LENTO
gone Poor Bess for his sake a garland will make my music shall be a groan. I'll
lay me down and die within some hollow tree The rav'n and cat the owl and bat shall
war...... ble forth my elegy did you not see my love as he past
by you? His two flaming eyes if they come nigh you they will scorch up your
2073

ALLEGRO MODERATO.
RECIT:
hearts Ladies beware ye lest he should dart a glance that may ensnare ye Hark
hark I hear old Charon bawl his boat he will no longer stay The furies lash their
MODERATO.
whips and cry come come away come come away Poor Bess will return to the
place whence she came since the world is so mad she can hope for no cure for

love's grown a bubble a shadow a name which fools do admire and wise men en....
Ad Lib:
VIVACE.
....dure cold and hungry am I grown Am....brosia will I feed upon drink nectar
pp
f
CON SPIRITO.
still and sing   Who is content does all sorrow prevent and Bess in her
Ad Lib.
straw while free from the Law in her thoughts is as great   great as a king.
Colla Voce
2073

Ex: 288.
Recit:
Oratorio of Samson by Handel
This day a solemn feast to Dagon held Relieves me from my
task of servile toil unwillingly their superstition yields this
rest to breathe heav'ns air fresh blowing pure and sweet task of servile toil Sweet
Ex: 289.
Ex: 290
Second part of "Return O God of Hosts". Samson. Handel.
Ex: 291.
2073.

Chorus from a Mass by Sebastian Bach.
Largo
Ground Bass

14
Ex: 29.
Chœr "Que d'attraits"
Iphigenie Gluck.
Andante Grazioso
pp
f
D.C.
2073

Ex: 294.
Un poco Adagio.
Haydn.
Tasto
Tasto
Tasto
2073